# SELF-AWARENESS WORKBOOK FOR KIDS 8-12

35+ Self-regulation Strategies to Improve Positive Thinking, Personal Strength, Mindfulness, and Social and Communication Skills

By

M. O'Reilly

Prime Pen Publisher

## ABOUT THE AUTHOR

M. O'Reilly is a professional psychologist and author. She is dedicated to supporting children in acquiring fundamental communication and social skills that will enable them to flourish as independent individuals. She committed herself to helping children successfully providing strategies for life-long positive results.

# CONTENTS

# CHAPTER 6: GOAL-SETTING AND ACHIEVING SUCCESS THROUGH SELF-REGULATION

# A LETTER TO PARENTS

First of all, thank you for your dedication to supporting your child's social and emotional development. I want to ensure that your kid, who is afraid of making mistakes, will develop into a self-regulated, assured, and high-achieving person.

Many kids lack self-awareness when they lack the proper tools and techniques. This limited way of thinking prevents kids from realizing their full potential. With effort and persistence, our skills and talents can develop or change. Self-regulated kids can overcome obstacles, tackle negativity, and handle social situations better. It also raises self-esteem.

This book explains to kids the importance of positive thinking, mindfulness, and social and communication skills. The activities in this book are made to help kids develop personal growth. They include making amends for errors, approaching problems from different angles, utilizing feedback, setting goals, and optimistic thinking.

I urge your kid to begin the exercises right away. Be excited and supportive along the process! They will be if you are, too!

# INTRODUCTION

*Emily had always had a negative outlook on life. She had the propensity to see the worst in every circumstance. She used to sit and think of everything that may go wrong.*

*Although Emily's parents did their best to uplift her positive side of life, it appeared as if their efforts were in vain.*

*Emily's class was going to a zoo trip one day. At first, Emily was thrilled, but then her mind began to rush with anxiety. "What if there would be dangerous animals around?" "What if I would get lost?"*

*Emily's classmates were excited as they entered the zoo, pointing at various animals and rushing to view the exhibits. Yet Emily hung back, worried. She was unwilling to leave the group for too long.*

*As the day passed, Emily's teacher noticed her behavior and pulled her aside for a conversation. "I know it can be intimidating to try new things or visit new places, Emily, but I believe everything will work out okay."*

*When she noticed the happiness on her friends' faces, she began to feel relaxed. Emily's disposition started to change. She started to see the world with a new perspective. She even made a new friend.*

*Emily was happy as they got on the bus to return to school. She experienced excitement and optimism about herself. She was aware that, occasionally, she would still have unfavorable thoughts, but she was also confident in her ability to overcome them and appreciate the beauty of her surroundings.*

*You can also change your perspective, like Emily.*

What if I tell you that you can overcome all of your difficulties? All you require is a mindset, a self-regulating mindset. Your brain may change if you start by knowing who you are! Your skills and talents can change with effort. That means you can do just about whatever you want. I will teach you to overcome obstacles and keep trying when things become difficult. The opportunities are infinite when you adopt a growth attitude.

There are a lot of enjoyable activities and exercises that will teach you how to practice self-regulation. Get into the world of self-awareness and be AWESOME!

# CHAPTER 1: UNDERSTANDING SELF-AWARENESS

Self-awareness is the capacity to know your thoughts, feelings, and behaviors. You may improve your self-awareness and ability to be purposeful, sympathetic, and effective. In this chapter, you will learn about self-awareness and why it's important for you. So let's start your journey of self-discovery and begin living a more authentic and fulfilling life!

# 1.1 GETTING TO KNOW MYSELF

*Henry had always had trouble controlling his emotions.*

*He was short-tempered. He had a problem getting along with his family and friends. His mother tried to help him learn anger management techniques, but it didn't seem like anything was working.*

*One day, Henry was playing with his brother when his brother accidentally knocked over his tower of blocks. Henry yelled at him. He was aware that he had made a mistake.*

*He was ashamed of his actions. His parents sat down and talked to him. He said, "I don't know why I become so angry," he said. "Even while I try to avoid doing that, there are situations when it's unavoidable."*

*After the attentive listening, his father suggested him to try deep breathing.*

*Henry initially hesitated. His father reassured him that it might help him constructively deal with his anger issues.*

*He began to practice the techniques and paid attention to his breathing. He experienced a wave of calmness. He experienced a sense of emotional control.*

*The weeks passed, and Henry's anger problems gradually started to disappear. He occasionally became angry but now he knew how to control his emotions. Even better, he began to enjoy breathing exercises.*

*Thinking back on that day when he yelled at his brother helped him a lot. He understood that he was adaptable and that, with time and effort, he could improve and become a better version of himself.*

*Do you know where you went wrong, like Henry?*

Being self-aware is like possessing a certain ability to comprehend yourself better. It aids in your awareness of your attributes, flaws, feelings, and thoughts. Imagine having x-ray vision like a superhero and being able to peep inside your head! Self-awareness allows you to use your knowledge to make wise decisions and comprehend why you feel the way you do.

*Alex struggled to interact with others.*

*He was an introverted, shy kid who wanted to play by himself. He struggled to make friends at school and frequently felt excluded from social activities.*

*Alex's parents signed him up for a public speaking course after noticing that he was having trouble in socializing. Alex's communication abilities improved due to the program, although he still struggled to talk in front of others.*

*Alex grew increasingly irritated with his poor communication skills as he grew older. He would frequently withdraw into his world, avoiding social interactions and experiencing loneliness. Alex was reluctant and reclusive despite his parents' best efforts to persuade him to make friends and participate in activities that would improve his communication abilities.*

*One day, Alex decided to participate in his school's talent competition. He had always had a passion for drawing, and his work was impressive. He was anxious as he took the stage but determined to show off his talent.*

*He wasn't expecting the audience to be so entranced. They were astounded by his intricate and exquisite work, and when he was done, they cheered. Alex experienced the first time in his life being truly seen and valued for who he was.*

*Following the talent show, Alex's classmates approached him and asked him questions to get to know him better. The fact that he had something special to contribute, that people were interested in what he had to say, and that he didn't need to be fearful of speaking with others were all realizations for Alex.*

*After that, Alex gradually began to come out of his shell. He started participating more in social events, and his self-assurance increased as he became aware of his ability to elicit a response from others through his art. Even though speaking in front of others was still difficult for him, he had discovered a way to express himself that felt genuine and significant.*

*In the end, Alex understood that effective communication only sometimes requires verbal exchange. It doesn't matter if you say the right thing or have the loudest voice in the room. Finding a means to express yourself that feels authentic to who you are and interacting meaningfully with others are the key.*

*Do you know who you are like Alex? If not, wear the Detective Cap.*

Being self-aware is like playing the role of a detective. You do not have to solve crimes. You are learning all the great aspects that make you, YOU! You can know yourself by paying attention to your thoughts, feelings, and behaviors, much like a detective needs to collect evidence and clues.

For instance, you enjoy playing soccer. You may have come to this conclusion because you get a rush of excitement each time you kick a ball. Or perhaps you have realized that you are usually happiest outside, in the presence of nature. These hints can be used to determine your passions and what makes you happy.

Use all of your clues to create a portrait of who you are. This can be accomplished by making a vision board, a collage of images, words, and symbols that express your goals, values, and aspirations. You may cut out images of your favorite pastimes, motivational sayings, or icons that reflect your character.

It enables you to make decisions that are true to who you are. For instance, if you are an introvert, you will prefer reading a book over a crowded party. Or, if you are aware of your enthusiasm for environmental preservation, you can volunteer for a beach cleaning rather than visiting the mall.

So get your detective cap and begin discovering all the fascinating aspects of who you are. The first step to leading a happy and meaningful life is to know who you are and then go for self-regulation.

## 1.2 WHY DO I NEED SELF-REGULATION SKILLS?

I want you to meet some children and hear their stories.

*Daisy: Not an Early Riser*

Let's hear the dilemma of Daisy, who is always late for school.

Daisy: "Good morning, Mom."

Mom: "Good morning, Daisy. You are running late again. You must hurry up if you don't want to be late for school."

Daisy (Rolling her eyes): "I know, Mom. But I couldn't sleep last night. And you know I always have trouble getting up in the morning."

Mom: "That's not a good excuse, Daisy. You need to learn to manage your time better. You can't keep being late for school every day. It's not fair to your teachers, and it's not fair to your classmates."

Daisy: "I know, Mom. I am sorry. But I just can't seem to help it. It's like my body won't let me wake up in the morning."

Mom: "Well, maybe you must start going to bed earlier. You can't stay up all night and expect to be awake and alert in the morning. Moreover, you need to set your alarm clock earlier, so you have enough time to get ready."

Daisy: "I guess you are right, Mom. But it's not just the mornings. I have trouble with time management all day long. I always seem to be running late."

Mom: "Well, maybe you need to start keeping a schedule. Write down all your activities and when you need to do them. That way, you will know what you need to do and when you need to do it."

Daisy: (nodding) "That's a good idea, Mom. I will try that. But can you help me? I am not very good at organizing my time."

Mom: "Of course, Daisy. I am always here to help you. But you need to take responsibility for your actions. You can't keep blaming your procrastination on other things. You need to be accountable for your time management."

Daisy: (smiling) "Thanks, Mom. I will do my best. I don't want to be late for school anymore."

## Do you also struggle with time like Daisy?

There is a lot to do between homework, hobbies, and having free time to play. Yet, even though most children don't have the cognitive abilities to independently arrange their schedules, you may learn how to prioritize and plan your time. Children who are taught time management skills at a young age internalize them. This ability prepares you for success throughout your lives.

Need help knowing where to start? Not to worry. To help you make this easier and more enjoyable, I will give you advice and some useful strategies.

## Liam: The Curious Soul

Let's hear the conversation between Liam and his mother.

Liam: "Mom, why do I need self-regulating skills?"

Mother: "Self-regulation is a superpower that allows you to manage your thoughts and feelings.

Liam: "Superpower? Cool! Why, then, is it significant?"

Mother: "It's crucial because it enables you to maintain composure and improves your focus. It helps you get along with people and makes you a kind person."

Liam: "Ah, I see now. But what if I am powerless over my emotions?"

Mother: "That's alright; developing self-regulation abilities needs practice. When you are unhappy, you can practice calming tactics like deep breathing, just like you practice football to grow better. It will get simpler to control your emotions with time."

Liam: "I will try it."

Mother: "Self-control, on the other hand, aids in fostering good relationships with others. You are less likely to say or do hurtful things to others. You can cooperate more successfully and communicate more efficiently."

Liam: "Wow, I never gave that much thought. I wish to have good self-control!"

Mother: "Wonderful, my boy. Keep in mind that you can master these skills with time and effort. Also, it will benefit you in many aspects of your life, including friendships, sports, and school."

*Do you want that superpower too?*

Self-regulation is a tool that gives you the power to manage your emotions and actions. When things become challenging or irritating, it's like having the ability to stop time and take a big breath. It enables you to think critically and maintain focus on your objectives. Self-awareness and self-regulation work together to help you become a confident and successful child, just like Batman needs Robin to help him rescue the day.

So, get ready; we are going to do some fun activities!

# CHAPTER 2: BUILDING POSITIVE THINKING

*Noah was an adventurous and curious child who adored discovering new things. He constantly desired to learn and explore new avenues but also struggled with self-doubt and negative beliefs. Even though he gave it his all, he frequently felt disappointed and discouraged.*

*As Noah's mother realized his difficulties, she decided to teach him the value of positive thinking. She made him realize that by altering our beliefs, we could alter our feelings, behaviors, and life.*

*This idea sounded interesting to Noah, so he decided to attempt it. He decided to fight any negativity that could have entered his head and replace them with constructive ones. He thought, "I may not be great yet, but with practice, I will get better," as opposed to "I will never be good at this."*

*Initially, Noah found it difficult to maintain his optimism, but as he practiced more, he started to experience developments in his life. He was more eager to take chances and attempt new things since he felt more secure. Even his interpersonal interactions improved due to his upbeat attitude and outgoing nature.*

*As Noah developed his capacity for optimistic thinking, he also gained a reputation for his contagious enthusiasm and positive outlook. Noah now realizes that cultivating positive thinking has advantages for himself and others. He appreciated his mother's advice and resolved to practice positive thinking techniques.*

Our mentality significantly impacts dealing with negativity and positivity in our life. I want you to confront your mind and take a big and significant risk. By making the changes mentioned in this chapter, your life will become far more consistent. Each activity will guarantee more self-awareness and self-regulation.

# ACTIVITY 1: FINDING THE MONSTER!

*You need to find the monster. Do you know its name? It is called 'Negativity.'*

The best thing in life is changing your perspective on the world. You will stop thinking about how miserable you have been all day. You will become aware of how frequently you would make bad decisions.

You will keep having bad thoughts running through your head. Consider creating time for thinking if you wish to avoid this. You need to become conscious of your negative attitude. Only then you will find the way out.

You should find your monster, become more conscious of your mindset, and change it.

## NEGATIVE THOUGHT MONSTER

Here are some examples of negative thoughts:

*"I am not good enough."*

*"No one likes me."*

*"I always mess things up."*

- Imagine what kind of monster would represent these negative thoughts.
- Be creative and describe the monster's appearance, personality, and behavior.

Now name some positive thoughts or actions, such as

*"I will learn from my mistakes,"*

*"I have friends who care about me,"*

*"I can take a break and do something I enjoy."*

Add these positive thoughts or actions to the monster's story, such as a superhero who defeats the monster or a friend who helps the monster become kinder and happier.

Negative thoughts can be like monsters that try to scare or hurt us. But just like we can defeat a monster in a story or game, we can also learn to defeat negative thoughts in real life.

# ACTIVITY 2: APPRECIATING MY PROGRESS

*Thinking about your progress is a great idea.*

It is a powerful tool for envisioning your successes. It builds a positive mindset. The simplest way is to reflect on your most recent accomplishments. Even if you haven't achieved "success" yet, keep thinking this way.

You will find it much simpler to keep on track when you are discouraged about your success and progress. You would have to make small adjustments. You will learn to ignore the negative aspects of your life.

You will be much more proud of your development. Keep in mind that changing anything positive takes time, even your own mindset!

## A PROGRESS TREE

Make a list of things you have learned or accomplished recently, such as reading a new book, solving a math problem, or making a new friend.

- Draw a tree trunk and branches on a piece of paper.
- Be creative and decorate the tree with leaves, flowers, or other ornaments.
- The tree represents your progress and growth, just like a real tree that grows taller and stronger over time.

Write some of your recent achievements or challenges on the leaves or flowers.

# ACTIVITY 3: LOOKING INTO MY POSITIVITY

*How frequently do you genuinely recall being optimistic in your mind?*

Express your positivity. You can do this only if you learn to find them. Looking at a joyful memory for five minutes is a fantastic approach to shift your perspective from negative to positive.

You can begin your day with a smile rather than a frown. Think back on something that happened in your life.

It's entirely acceptable if you decide that you don't need this at all in your life. Reflecting on a positive event might help you feel more at ease with who you are and where you are heading.

## MY POSITIVE TRAITS

Remember the time when you felt proud of yourself. This could be something you achieved, a compliment you received, or a fun experience.

- Write about that moment.
- Think about some of your positive qualities. Examples could include kindness, creativity, humor, perseverance, or bravery.
- Write down the space below, using a different color for each.

By reflecting on your positive traits, you can gain greater self-awareness and appreciation for your unique qualities. You will feel confident and resilient in facing challenges.

# ACTIVITY 4: CHALLENGING MY THOUGHTS

*Do you challenge your limited thoughts once in a while?*

If not, do it now. You will be able to keep evolving if you challenge your preconceptions.

It's quite simple to never question our views and presumptions, but doing so could be unnecessarily pessimistic. Instead, consider whether that line of thought is valid and why it exists.

Whenever you notice your thoughts spiraling downward in a negative direction, become active and seek the issue that concerns you. Is your first assumption or thought still true today?

Many kids avoid taking this path because they prefer to avoid being corrected. Yet being incorrect is not a bad thing—just it's another opportunity to learn!

This will make you less entrenchment and less prone to feel threatened by disagreement.

# I LOVE CHALLENGING MY THOUGHTS BECAUSE THIS IS HOW I WILL GET BETTER.

## IS THAT THOUGHT TRUE?

Write down a negative or unhelpful thought you have been having recently.

Examples could include "I am not good enough," "Everyone is always judging me," or "I will never be able to do this."

Write down whether this thought is true or not.

Think about alternative, more balanced thoughts that could replace negative thoughts.

For example, instead of "I am not good enough," you could think ", I may not be perfect, but I have many strengths and talents."

Decorate the space with colors or stickers to make it more visually appealing.

## ACTIVITY 5: LEARNING FROM MY FAILURES

Many of us are aware of our failure, but why?

Finding answers will be a lot simpler if you take the time to consider why you failed.

Just take a seat and list your failures. Now that you are aware of what needs improvement, you may move forward with it even though it may be painful.

Try it again every time you fail because doing so will simplify your life. Choose the route to failure, not failure itself!

If you don't try to change this, get ready for low self-esteem. Solutions are made possible by looking back at failure.

Continuing on the right path will be much simpler if you examine and analyze your successes and failures. Also, it will significantly raise the likelihood of locating a durable answer.

# LEARNING FROM MY FAILURES

## My Failure

### What happened?

### My learning for the future

# LEARNING FROM MY FAILURES

Look at this wheel and color the part that applies to you.

# ACTIVITY 6: CELEBRATING MY SUCCESSES

*Many kids find it difficult to accept achievement. Well! They should not.*

If you feel this way, ask your loved ones to respond honestly the next time this thought crosses your mind.

Be ready to sense a confidence crisis. It's a risky issue that will only make you feel worse. Asking whenever it's on will help you avoid it.

While focusing only on your failures, you will continue undermining your accomplishments. This fosters negativity. It is the opposite of what a positive and self-regulated life requires.

You will grow more at ease with yourself and be conscious of your life's victories and setbacks.

## CELEBRATING MY SUCCESSES

Note some of your accomplishments on the images below. This could be learning how to ride a bike, scoring a goal in your favorite game, performing well on a task, being a nice friend, or discovering something new!

## ACTIVITY 7: ACCEPTING A NEW CHALLENGE

*How frequently do you accept a new challenge?*

This is a highly effective approach to guarantee that there is always a challenge for you.

Difficulties are excellent for teaching us important life lessons. Find out your strengths and talents.

You do not need to mistrust your capacity to pick up new knowledge and abilities. You can increase your general understanding by accepting new challenges.

# ACCEPTING A NEW CHALLENGE

Knowing what challenges you will help you start to consider solutions. Go over each challenge and circle the ones that present the greatest difficulty for you.

| | | | |
|---|---|---|---|
| Writing | Reading | Listening | Getting along with others |
| Art | Following rules | Self-control | Punctuality |
| Sports | Speaking to someone | Focusing | Dancing |

Select one of the challenges you encircled. What can you do to tackle it?

_____

_____

_____

# CHAPTER 3: FEELING GOOD ABOUT MYSELF

*Natalia was a talented and imaginative kid who enjoyed singing, writing, and sketching.*

*She was constantly anxious to show off her inventions to others, although she frequently struggled with confidence in her skills. She was concerned that she was not good enough and was terrified of other people's opinions or judgement.*

*Natalia's teacher observed her reluctance to present her work and inquired about it. Natalia remarked that she lacked self-assurance and was terrified of what people would think. Her teacher calmly listened to her before explaining the idea of self-worth.*

*She emphasized the value of appreciating one's individual qualities, talents, and successes, no matter how modest. She exhorted Natalia to concentrate on her development and have self-confidence.*

*Natalia focused more on her accomplishments after taking her teacher's advice. She kept journals of her writings, music, and illustrations and was proud of every entry. Being aware that she had put a lot of effort into it and represented her special creativity, she also started to present her work to others with more assurance.*

*Natalia had more self-assurance.*

Being content and sure of who you mean, you feel good about yourself. It's critical to remember that each person is distinctive and exceptional in their own way. You can feel good about yourself by being kind to others, giving everything you have, and concentrating on your abilities.

It's also acceptable to make errors and grow from them. Keep in mind to enjoy your successes and feel pleased with yourself. In this chapter, I will teach you how to achieve it through activities.

# ACTIVITY 8: RECOGNIZING MY SPECIAL GIFTS

*Everyone has unique abilities and skills that set them apart from others.*

While some people are excellent at sports or cracking jokes, others excel at painting. No matter how tiny or big they may seem, it's crucial to acknowledge and enjoy our own unique gifts.

Using those talents, we may influence the world and make others happy. So always keep in mind that you are unique and that you have incredible talents!

## SPECIAL GIFTS COLLAGE

- Think about your talents or special gifts. For example, are you good at drawing, playing sports, making friends, telling jokes, etc.? Write down your answers on a separate piece of paper.
- Next, look through the magazines or printed images to find pictures that represent your special gifts.
- Find images that may not directly relate to your gifts but inspire you.
- Once you have a collection of images, cut them out and make a collage.
- Glue the images down onto the paper.
- Use markers or crayons to add details or decorations to your collage.

# ACTIVITY 9: ACCEPTING MYSELF

*Loving and valuing who you are as you entail acceptance of who you are.*

You are distinctive, and one of a kind, and nobody else is precisely like you! Even though we may occasionally feel inadequate or wish we were someone else, it's crucial to realize these thoughts are unfounded.

Accept your strengths and weaknesses since they define who you are! You will be happier and more self-assured when you embrace and adore yourself. Therefore, constantly keep in mind to love yourself and accept who you are.

## TREASURE HUNT

You are going on a treasure hunt to discover things about yourself.

Be open and curious as you search for treasures within yourself.

Write down the following categories in the space given below.

- Something you are good at
- Something you like about the appearance
- Something you appreciate about your personality
- Something you are proud of
- Something that makes you unique

Take some time to reflect on each category.

## ACTIVITY 10: PRACTICING KINDNESS

*Be kind to everyone, whether they are members of your family, friends, or strangers.*

Being friendly to people and making them happy are examples of kindness. You can exhibit compassion by using nice words, sharing toys, assisting someone, or simply smiling at them.

You share happiness and improve the world by being kind to others. Remember that acts of kindness are contagious and can motivate several other people to follow suit.

### KINDNESS ROCKS

- Take small rocks and paint them with colorful designs or positive messages using acrylic paint and paintbrushes.
- Be creative and use your imagination.
- While the rock is drying, brainstorm the kind acts you can do for others, such as helping a neighbor with their groceries, writing a thank-you note to a teacher, or simply smiling and saying hello to someone who looks lonely.
- Once the rocks are dry, go outside and leave your painted rocks in places where someone might find them.
- These rocks will serve as a reminder to whoever finds them that kindness is all around them.

## ACTIVITY 11: OFFERING MY HELP

A significant approach to expressing love and support is by helping others.

Being willing to help someone in need indicates that you are offering your assistance. You can assist in various ways, such as helping a friend, volunteering to carry someone's bag, or assisting your parents with household duties.

You may make someone feel loved and respected when you provide your assistance. Keep in mind that even modest deeds of kindness impact someone's life.

Hence, always be prepared to provide a helping hand, and you will improve the world.

# IT TAKES COURAGE TO BE KIND.

## HELPING HANDS

- Think about when you needed help, and someone was there for you.

- Talk to an adult about how it made you feel to receive help and why it's important to help others.

- Do at least one thing during the day to help someone else. It could be something helping a friend with their homework or offering to carry something heavy for someone.

- Write down or draw what they did to help someone and how it made them feel.

- Take time to reflect on the activity with the child at the end of the day, and discuss how small acts of kindness can make a big difference in someone's day.

- This activity teaches you the value of helping others, developing empathy, and building social skills.

# ACTIVITY 12: MAKING MY FAMILY HAPPY

*Your family is your home!*

You may do a lot of things to make your family happy. You can assist your parents with household duties like laundry folding and table arranging. You can spend time with your siblings engaging in activities or playing games.

You can also embrace your family members and tell them that you love them. Making your family happy makes you happy as well! Always remember that treating your family with love and care can help you forge lasting bonds and make wonderful memories as a family.

## HAPPINESS CARD

- Think about what makes your family happy. It could be spending time together, doing something fun or helping each other.
- Make a "Happiness Card" for each family member.
- Fold a piece of paper in half to create a card.
- Use markers or crayons to draw pictures, write messages, or decorate the card however they like.
- Write something nice about each family member on your card. For example, you could write, "Thank you for always making me laugh" or "I love spending time with you".
- Present your cards to your family members and explain why you made them.
- Take time to reflect on the activity and discuss how it made your family members feel.
- This activity teaches you the value of expressing gratitude and kindness toward your family members. It will also help you develop your creativity and communication skills.

# ACTIVITY 13: USING MY TIME PRODUCTIVELY

*Using your time productively means doing things that are significant and beneficial.*

While it's necessary to unwind and enjoy yourself, utilizing your time mindfully is equally crucial. You can make good use of your free time by reading books, engaging in a pastime, completing homework, or picking up a new skill.

When you use your time well, you feel accomplished and proud of yourself. Remember that time is precious, and you can maximize it by engaging in meaningful and helpful activities.

## MY PRODUCTIVE DAY

- Think about your typical daily routine.
- Please list tasks or activities you would like to complete in a day to make it productive.
- Prioritize your list and make a schedule for your day. You should include time for each task or activity and breaks for meals and rest.
- Follow your schedule for the day and mark off each completed task or activity.
- Reflect on your day.
- By doing this activity, you will learn time management and achieve your goals. It will also help you develop your planning and organizational skills.

# ACTIVITY 14: TAKING MY RESPONSIBILITIES

*Being accountable for your actions entails taking responsibility.*

It's crucial to own up to your errors and set the record straight. By accepting responsibility, you demonstrate your dependability and reliability.

You may be accountable by owning up to your mistakes, offering an apology, and trying to make things right. You may demonstrate responsibility by finishing your tasks on time, doing your homework, and abiding by the rules at school and home.

Accepting responsibility is crucial to maturing into a respectable and responsible family member.

## MY RESPONSIBILITY LEAVES

Taking responsibility can help you become more independent and trustworthy.

Draw a tree trunk.

Cut leaf shapes from paper.

Think of different responsibilities you have in your daily life, such as completing your homework, cleaning your room, or helping with chores.

Write each responsibility on a leaf shape and attach it to the branches of your tree.

Reflect on each responsibility and think about why it's important.

This activity teaches you the importance of taking responsibility for your actions and how they can positively impact your life. It will also help you develop your creativity and critical thinking skills.

# CHAPTER 4: DEVELOPING MINDFULNESS SKILLS

David's parents observed that he had trouble concentrating.

He used to easily get distracted. He had anger issues too. After hearing about it, they chose to learn more about the idea of mastering mindfulness.

David's mother once taught the benefits of mindfulness to him over dinner. She explained to him the importance of focusing on the here and now. David was curious and wished that he knew more.

They began by working on basic breathing techniques together. David would observe the sensations of his breath as it entered and left his body while remaining still. He initially struggled to remain still and concentrated, but with time and effort, he improved.

*David's parents observed a significant difference in him. He appeared more collected and at peace, and his ability to focus on his studies and other tasks improved. He even began to appreciate his surroundings.*

*David's newly acquired mindfulness abilities had a good effect on his interactions with others in addition to helping him. He had greater empathy and comprehension and started expressing his wants and feelings to others around him.*

*David's practice of mindfulness eventually integrated itself into his daily routine. He could appreciate life's basic joys in a way he had never been before because he was no longer plagued by distraction or restlessness.*

*He appreciated the lessons his parents had imparted to him and knew practicing mindfulness would bring him contentment.*

You should control your emotions if you want to succeed. Yet getting to this point can be difficult for most kids. So, I've outlined some of the strategies in this chapter. A solid mindful living is crucial for a stable, secure way of living.

Try the ideas and suggestions below to help balance and calm your monkey mind. Make yourself as influential in your life as you possibly can!

# ACTIVITY 15: IDENTIFYING MY NEGATIVE EMOTIONS

*Do you find it challenging to express and comprehend your emotions?*

Identifying your negative emotions is important.

It may only take a slight change in perspective to make it simpler to solve a problem quickly.

Change is difficult, but the biggest benefit is that it makes it possible for you to understand how you truly feel.

You will become more capable of thinking things out before acting, which makes you less likely to respond badly to a situation.

## YOUR TURN

Sometimes, we experience emotions that are not pleasant, such as anger, grief, or frustration. It's critical to recognize these feelings to comprehend their causes.

Here is what you need to do:

- Recall a moment when you were angry or frustrated.
- What happened? or How did it make you feel?
- Create a drawing of the unpleasant emotion in your drawing book. For instance, if you were upset, you may depict a volcano or a storm cloud in your drawing.
- Name the emotion when you have finished drawing.
- Repetition of this practice can help you understand your feelings and how to express them healthily.
- Be comfortable and honest while doing this activity.
- You can keep a separate drawing book for this activity.

# ACTIVITY 16: HANDLING MY NEGATIVE EMOTIONS

*The mind and the spirit should deal with bad feelings.*

Figure out why these negative emotions exist.

Life becomes a lot simpler when you understand that negative emotions are momentary moods.

Your emotions will shape your day. So, make the change. Make it less probable for unpleasant emotions to disturb you because you know they will eventually pass.

## SKETCH THE SOLUTION

It's crucial to learn how to deal with negative emotions. It's normal to experience them.

Here is what you need to do:

- Recall a negative emotion, such as sadness or anger.
- What happened? or How did it make you feel?

- Sketch an image of a healthy method to deal with that emotion in your sketchbook.

- For instance, if you were upset, you may sketch a picture of yourself exhaling or walking to defuse the situation.

- Consider concrete solutions, such as talking to a trusted friend or engaging in a favorite activity.

- Repetition of this activity will teach you good coping mechanisms for unhealthy emotions.

## ACTIVITY 17: MINDFUL WALKING

*This type of meditation makes it simpler to achieve mental clarity.*

With mindful walking, you would be less prone to make mistakes that may have been prevented.

**YOUR TURN**

Mindful walking is a method of paying attention to each step you take. It helps you to be present and aware of your surroundings.

Follow the steps:

- Choose a park or a peaceful area where you can stroll.
- Take it easy and concentrate on each step you take while you walk.
- Concentrate on the feeling of your feet making contact with the earth.
- Observe how it feels about raising and planting each foot and the sensation of the ground beneath you.
- Pay attention to what you hear and see in your surroundings.
- Concentrate on your breath.
- Keep walking consciously as long as you are comfortable.

Make sure the activity is enjoyable and stimulating so that you will feel at ease while practicing mindful walking.

# ACTIVITY 18: DEEP BREATHING

*Deep breathing will enable you to calm down, assess your situation, and respond maturely and logically.*

Breathe deeply and slowly.

Every single day, if you master this breathing method, you will want to practice it constantly. It's a fantastic way to unwind and temporarily escape from your problems.

It enables you to approach challenges analytically. After making this change, you will feel sharper, happier, and healthier.

# DEEP BREATHING

Trace the number 8 with your finger, breath in the beginning of the number. Breath out towards the end.

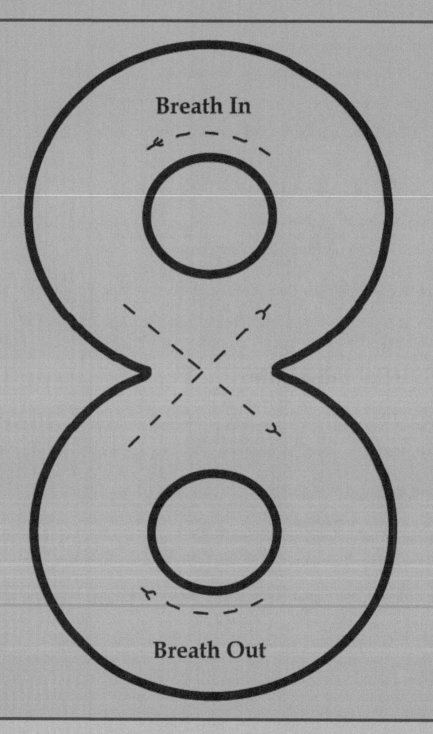

# ACTIVITY 19: MINDFUL EATING

*Do you acknowledge the important role that food plays in our lives?*

The concept is straightforward: consider how much you eat affects your feelings. After all, what we eat affects how we feel throughout the day!

Make brief notes on how you felt and the foods you consumed. Keep track of how your act of eating influences or restricts your emotions and whether that needs to change.

But eating well makes life simpler! Your body will undoubtedly function better during the day if you provide the correct nutrients and support.

Dealing with issues and negativity will be easier if we nourish our bodies properly.

## APPRECIATE EACH BITE

Appreciate each bite of your food while being completely present and aware of what you eat.

Here is what you need to do:

- Settle down and enjoy the meal or snack.
- Pause and observe the food, noticing its flavors, colors, and textures.
- Take a tiny mouthful and concentrate on how the food feels.
- Pay attention to the food's warmth.
- Take your time and enjoy every bite of food.
- Notice any ideas or sensations that arise when you are eating.
- Then bring your attention back to the food and notice your feelings and thoughts without passing judgement.
- Talk to your parents and tell them how you feel after your meal.

# ACTIVITY 20: CHANGING MY PERSPECTIVE

*Take a step back and think!*

When pessimism dominates, step back and consider the bigger picture. It will help you appreciate both success and failure.

This is important since it's so simple to do.

When you don't feel you can develop any optimism, do this. Putting things in perspective allows us to see how much we exaggerate things.

Life would be difficult right now if we didn't undergo this transformation!

## YOUR TURN

changing your perspective can aid in developing empathy and understanding of others.

Here is what you need to do:

- Consider an issue you are currently dealing with, such as a disagreement with a friend or a difficulty at school.
- Get into great detail about that issue.
- After you have recounted the circumstance, consider how another person would perceive it. For instance, if you disagree with a buddy, you would try to imagine what your friend might be thinking or experiencing.
- Ask yourself hypothetical questions like, "What if you were in your friend's shoes?" This will encourage you to consider many viewpoints. Or "How would a stranger perceive this issue?"
- Consider how this exercise has affected your perspective.
- Talk to an adult and ask their opinion.

# ACTIVITY 21: STRETCHING TIME

*Stretching is one of the most effective strategies for you to improve your state of fitness.*

Simply getting out of bed allows you to stretch your arms, neck, back, legs, calves, and hamstrings.

It lets you calm down without experiencing all the aches and pains most of us experience throughout the day. It is extremely helpful for promoting physical recovery from pain.

You will wake up less tired and accomplish your daily goals without experiencing any side effects.

## TOE TOUCH

Toe touching is a simple stretch for you that is easy to complete. This stretch focuses on the muscles in the legs, particularly the calves and hamstrings.

Follow the steps:

* Stand straight.
* Bend over at your waist, and reach with your feet together for your toes.
* Stretch as far as you can comfortably go, even if you can't quite touch your toes.
* You can also do it in a sitting position.
* Cross your legs in front of you.
* Then stoop forward, bending as far as is comfortable or reaching for your toes.
* Both stretches require you to hold the stretch for 20 seconds before releasing it.

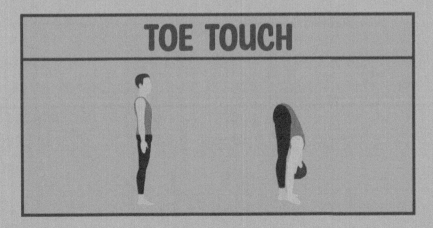

TOE TOUCH

## ARMS CIRCLE

Arms circle help in stretching the muscles of the shoulder and elbow joint, where the arm joins the shoulder.

Follow the steps:

Make a straight edge with your arms by holding them to the side.

Then make circles with your hands.

Start slowly, gradually getting bigger until those circles are large, then get smaller again.

Move slowly and draw circles anticlockwise after beginning with a clockwise motion.

# ARMS CIRCLE

## CHILD'S POSE

Child pose is among the top stretching exercises. It lowers your stress levels and soothes your muscles. It gives you a wonderful stretch and aids in relaxation.

Follow the steps:

- Kneel with your feet together and your knees slightly apart.
- Keep your head on the mat as you stoop forward to the ground.
- Your arms should be stretched in front of your head, palms outward.
- Your lower half should be moved so that your buttocks and heels meet.
- Slowly inhale and exhale.
- Take a few minutes to hold the stretch.
- Go back to the starting place.

**CHILD'S POSE**

# CHAPTER 5: MAKING AND KEEPING FRIENDS

Kate struggled to make friends since she was a quiet, shy child.

She battled with loneliness and frequently felt excluded during lunch and recess. Her parents became aware of her issues and decided to assist her in developing the ability to make and keep friends.

They began by explaining the meaning of a good friend to Kate. They emphasized the value of empathy, kindness, and listening to others. Although Kate paid close attention, she was still apprehensive about using these abilities in real life.

*Her parents advised her to begin by enlisting in an interest-based activity. She started meeting children who shared her interests and ambitions. When Kate decided to join the hockey club, she was surprised to learn that they had selected her.*

*Kate gradually got to know the other team members. She was apprehensive at first. They began to develop a bond of trust and friendship as they worked together.*

*Kate discovered that establishing and keeping friends required more than just being kind. It also required getting to know your friends and discovering points of shared interest.*

*It did boost her self-assurance. She was still reserved but had developed the confidence to approach strangers.*

Friendship plays a significant role in our lives. Relationships can be joyful for us. At first, making friends could seem intimidating, but it's much simpler than you imagine.

This chapter will provide you with some wonderful advice on making and keeping friends, whether you are starting at a new school or want to widen your social circle.

You will discover what makes a good buddy, how to strike up a discussion, and how to resolve disputes. So get ready to socialize and have a good time!

# ACTIVITY 22: CONTROLLING MY ANGER

*Everyone experiences anger, but learning how to regulate it is crucial.*

We may do or say things that we later regret while we're upset. For this reason, it's crucial to acquire some advice on controlling your rage constructively. This chapter will teach you several methods for managing your anger, including deep breathing exercises and talking to a trustworthy person.

If you learn to regulate your anger, you will handle social interactions more easily and uphold healthy connections with people.

# CONTROLLING MY ANGER

Sometimes we need to take a step back to control our anger. Choose which of the following activities would be a good break from your angry state of mind!

- Yoga

- Relax in a comfortable chair

- Practicing breathing

- Play with your pet

- Music

- Outdoor walking

- Coloring an art book

- Reading a book

Add your preferred anger-break strategy.

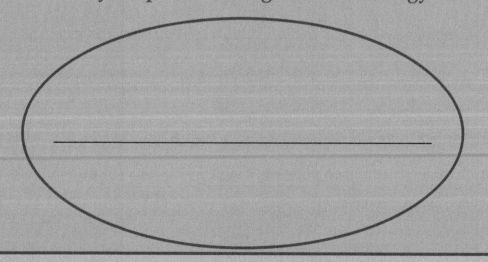

# ACTIVITY 23: COMMUNICATING MY CONCERNS

*Communication is essential in making and keeping friendships.*

It's critical to respectfully convey your opinions, feelings, and concerns. Using "I" statements, active listening, and maintaining your composure are just a few techniques for effectively conveying your concerns.

You will learn to forge greater connections with others and handle social situations with assurance. You learn how to express your worries healthily. So get prepared to master the art of expression!

## YOUR TURN

Here is what you need to do:

- Recall something that is worrying you.
- Express your concern by writing a letter or drawing a picture. This will enable you to creatively communicate your emotions.
- Once you have done your writing or drawing, talk to your parents or teacher and describe what you have made and how it relates to your worry.
- Ask for potential answers or approaches to dealing with your issues.
- Ask them to write a letter to you just like you did.

# ACTIVITY 24: USING MY POSITIVE HUMOR

*When it comes to interacting with others, humor is a powerful tool.*

Positive humor may improve relationships. It defuses uncomfortable circumstances and even lifts your spirits. This activity will advise how to use your good humor in social settings.

You should identify common ground, choose appropriate jokes, and avoid sarcasm. You can improve your relationships with people by effectively using positive humor. So get ready to show off your sense of humor!

# USING MY POSITIVE HUMOR

We frequently appear odd in pictures. Yet, you can make a picture funnier by adding an odd thing the subject would be thinking or saying. Take three of your friends' photos. Cut them to get them fit in the space below. Then, include something humorous but not hurtful that each friends might be considering or saying.

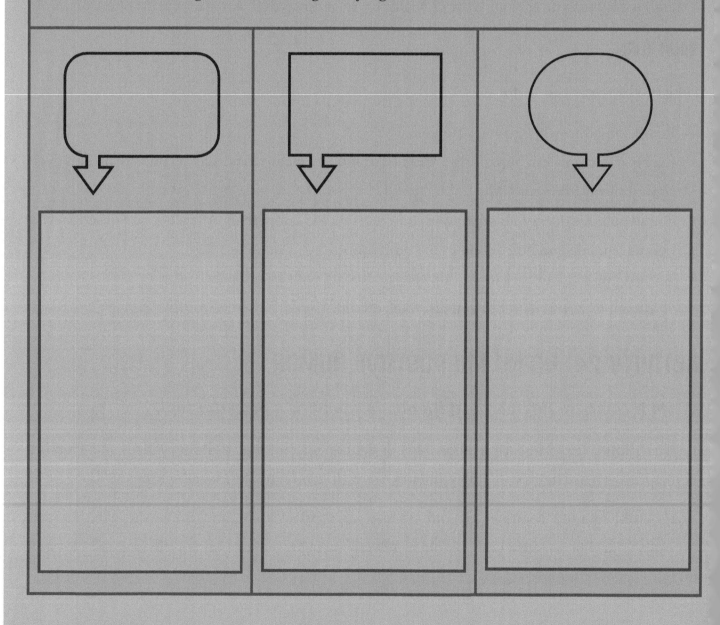

# ACTIVITY 25: SAYING 'NO' TO BULLYING

*Bullying is never acceptable. Thus it's crucial to learn how to refuse it.*

It's crucial to speak up and ask for support from a reliable adult if you are bullied. You need to learn several strategies to combat bullying, including maintaining composure, using assertive body language, and using your words.

You can make everyone's social environment safer and happier by learning to say "no" to bullying. Make a change and transform into a superhero that fights the bully!

## YOUR TURN

Here is your turn:

- Recall a time when you or your friend was the target of bullying.
- Express your feelings and views regarding the encounter before a trusted adult.
- After analyzing the problem, come up with some retorts for the bully.
- Ask your parents or teacher about what you could have done.
- Make a list of non-aggressive and non-confrontational responses to convey your feelings.
- Practice saying "No" in various contexts. For instance, if someone attempts to seize your toy or calls you a derogatory name.

# ACTIVITY 26: UNDERSTANDING MY FELLOWS

*We may create stronger bonds and have more fun with one another when we take the time to get to know one another.*

You need active listening and empathy to understand your fellows. Understanding other people will help you establish more solid bonds. It will help you make new acquaintances easier.

# UNDERSTANDING MY FELLOWS

It is clear from our body language what we mean. View the two children below. The girl exudes self-assurance and confidence. The boy exudes uncertainty and fear. List all the variations in their body language that you notice and write in the space given below.

_____

_____

_____

_____

# ACTIVITY 27: LEARNING TO COMPROMISE

*Finding a solution to satisfy everyone is a key to learning to compromise.*

It's normal when our desires differ from those of friends or family members. When we reach a compromise, we hear each other out and seek a resolution that benefits everyone.

For instance, if you want to play cricket and your friend wants to play basketball, you could agree to play both activities simultaneously or alternately. It is a terrific method to settle issues and have fun with your friends!

## A PAPER PUZZLE

Compromising is about coming up with a solution that benefits everyone.

Here is what you need to do:

- Recall an instance where you and your friend disagreed on what to do.
- Go to that friend and express your opinions and feelings regarding the circumstance.
- Think of three options that may benefit both of you.
- Write them on a piece of paper.
- Cut out the answers and mix them to make a paper puzzle.
- Reassemble the puzzle in a way that demonstrates the effectiveness of compromise.
- Invite your friend to discuss the merits of each solution and how you may collaborate to identify one that satisfies your shared needs.

# ACTIVITY 28: PRACTICING ACTIVE LISTENING

Active listening demands you to stop what you are doing, pay attention to the person speaking, and ask questions. Make sure you understand. You can also demonstrate that you are paying attention. When you listen to people with all your attention, it makes them feel important!

## YOUR TURN

Active listening is listening to what someone says while demonstrating your understanding and concern.

Here is what you need to do:

- Sit with one of your parents.
- Discuss a topic that interests them, such as a recent experience or a cherished activity.
- Encourage them to speak uninterrupted for two to three minutes.
- Maintain eye contact, nod, and ask questions to demonstrate interest and knowledge while your parent speaks.
- Change roles and repeat the task when your parent has finished speaking.
- Discuss with your parent how it felt to be listened to and how they felt.

# CHAPTER 6: GOAL-SETTING AND ACHIEVING SUCCESS THROUGH SELF-REGULATION

Jack liked soccer. He had aspirations of playing soccer and becoming a pro at it. Yet Jack understood that he would have to put in much effort and set goals to fulfil his dream of becoming a professional player.

Jack decided to jot down his goals one day. He noted that he wanted to increase his physical fitness, shooting precision, and dribbling ability. He also noted that he hoped to give the best performance among his team members.

*Jack understood that he had to put in a lot of effort and maintain the discipline to succeed. He created a routine for himself that included exercise and practice sessions. Also, Jack recognized that self-regulation meant having control over his thoughts, feelings, and behavior. He was aware that he would need to remain motivated and focused.*

*Jack started applying self-control strategies to his regular activities. He used positive self-talk, telling himself that he could accomplish it and could succeed in his objectives.*

*Jack's perseverance and commitment eventually paid off. His soccer abilities began to advance. He participated in competitions at school.*

*Jack understood that using self-regulation strategies and creating objectives enabled him to attain his dreams. He was filled with self-confidence and inspired to keep striving.*

Jack's story demonstrates the value of goal-setting and self-control as abilities that can aid people in leading successful lives. Everyone can realize their potential and achieve their goals with effort, commitment, and self-control.

Good lifestyle habits are sometimes taken for granted, but they can be a valuable quality to take into account. Ensure that your lifestyle can keep becoming better depending on your daily routines and goals. Each activity in this chapter will increase your productivity at home and school.

# ACTIVITY 29: WHAT IS MY PASSION?

*Have you identified your life passions?*

Find your goals, route, and ambitions in life. Does anything give you a butterfly feeling in your stomach? This emotion motivates us to learn more about who we are. Consider how the day will advance your pursuit of that passion each morning.

You will move from one day, week, and year to the next. You will better yourself and always have an optimistic mindset. You increase your chances of success since you are clear on your objectives passions and goals.

## WHAT IS MY PASSION?

## ACTIVITY 30: DEFINING MY VISION

The most influential people have a vision or a dream.

Ensure that you clearly understand where you want to go, including a successful role model. Following through with this is crucial because it guarantees your ongoing success. Implementing that step just entails spending the morning planning out your life's goals.

Knowing your life's dream and purpose is a powerful quality. Without identifying what motivates us, we muddle through each day. Yet, you will have consistent reactions and advancement if you make this change. You will be more motivated and actively interested in achieving your objectives.

## DEFINING MY VISION

Create a vision for yourself and put it down in writing. Put it in a location that you will see it every day. On the sticky note on this page, you can jot down ideas for your vision.

## ACTIVITY 31: I AM BIGGER THAN MY EXCUSES

Are you bigger than your excuses?

Do you look for justifications to avoid facing your failure? Focus on your mistakes to change them. You need to identify what went wrong, and how you can stop blaming others. As a child, I had a very uncertain life. I would feel vulnerable around everyone. Now that I can identify my flaws, I feel more at ease and optimistic than I previously did. You too can!

# I AM BIGGER THAN MY EXCUSES

### For each given statement and highlight your answer.

| | | |
|---|---|---|
| I just cannot do this task. | Excuse | Positive Thinking |
| I am not good at anything. | Excuse | Positive Thinking |
| I will learn it if I keep practicing. | Excuse | Positive Thinking |
| I will not give up. | Excuse | Positive Thinking |
| I am not good enough. | Excuse | Positive Thinking |
| I will ask for someone's help. | Excuse | Positive Thinking |
| I can improve if I self-regulate myself. | Excuse | Positive Thinking |
| There is no one to help me. | Excuse | Positive Thinking |

# ACTIVITY 32: INSPIRING MYSELF

*Thinking about all of your achievements is the simplest method to motivate yourself.*

How can you achieve that level of accomplishment? To accomplish this, all you need to do is to reflect on your past. Describe your journey there. How were you feeling? What prevents you from experiencing the same success today? Never stop looking for the answer to shape your future, planning for it, or preparing for it.

# ACTIVITY 33: MY PRIORITIES

*Setting your priorities will make it easier to go where you need to.*

Write down a list of the events that would take place the following day. Make rough timeframes for each. This will make your planning easier. Practice this at night. Observe how you responded to deadlines like this. Without this change, your life would be chaotic, with "good days" and "poor days," with schoolwork piling up until it would be practically difficult to handle later.

You can live a happy life since you become aware of the consistency of your days. Even though there are fewer "good days," the "terrible days" are over!

## MY PRIORITIES

### List your priorities in the boxes given below.

| Today | This Week |
|---|---|
| | |
| **This Month** | **This Year** |
| | |

# ACTIVITY 34: KEEP EXPLORING

*There is always more for us to learn.*

There are always new things to explore, locations, and experiences. You give your brain several possibilities to develop and evolve while maintaining curiosity.

## WAYS TO FEED YOUR CURIOSITY

- Read books. Getting knowledge is easy to do by reading. Nonfiction books can teach you about actual people and events, while fiction books can help you learn important lessons. Many of the world's most successful people have admitted that they do reading daily.

- Be mindful of others around you. See how others behave. Inquire about people's experiences. We may all benefit from one another.

- Don't be frightened to appear foolish. Kids frequently prevent themselves from trying new things because they are embarrassed or terrified of failing in front of others. Do not let this stop you! Just for attempting, most people will appreciate you.

- A fantastic way to satisfy your curiosity and gain new knowledge is through experimentation. Find out about safe scientific experiment ideas from your teacher or parents.

- Let your thoughts roam, and then follow where they lead you. Our minds are frequently intrigued even when we don't intend to be curious! Be mindful of your ideas. You could even put them in writing and further consider them later.

- Be aware of your surroundings. Consider focusing on the real world around you rather than a phone, tablet, or other technology. Take an interest in your surroundings.

- Visit zoos, aquariums, and museums. These are all excellent locations to pick up fresh information and pique your interest in a different subject.

- Keep thinking like a child! Children naturally exhibit curiosity since they have imaginations. Keep going!

## FILL YOUR BRAIN

Brainstorm everything you want to explore, and fill your brain picture.

# ACTIVITY 35: LEARNING TO LET GO

*Many of us, including myself, are constrained by our material possessions.*

It might not be easy, but you need to start letting go. Learn that life continues. Learn to let go of something valuable to you to a friend, member of your family, or charity. There's more to life than holding things tight! Let go of suspicion and pessimism. You will be free if you give it a try yourself.

## YOUR TURN

- Consider a negative or apprehensive thought you have been clinging to.
- Express your opinions and feelings regarding this circumstance.
- Write down what you want to let go of on a sheet of paper.
- This emotion or circumstance is symbolized by a word, a picture, or a symbol.
- Tightly grasp the paper while it is being crumpled.
- Stand up and visualize grasping a hefty object.
- Raise your hand, holding the paper above your head.
- Release the paper and let it fall to the ground.
- Take a big breath.
- Finally, discuss your feelings with your parent after letting go. Reiterate the idea that, despite being challenging, letting go can be liberating and uplifting. Adopt this daily habit that no longer serves you a purpose.

# ACTIVITY 36: STARTING MY DAY EARLY

*One of the best things my daughter has ever done was set her alarm for an hour earlier.*

Being up an hour earlier makes you more productive and gives you enough time to do your tasks. Make it a habit. It has been a cornerstone in bringing about every other constructive activity in this book. Life would continue to be stressful. By starting your day early, you will make yourself more productive. This self-regulating change will make it simple for you to begin working more consistently and optimistically.

## EARLY BIRD CATCHES THE WORM

You know the advantages of rising early, such as having extra time for breakfast, exercise, or getting ready for school. You might also give examples of successful individuals who are early risers, such as CEOs or athletes.

Here is what you need to do:

- Sketch a picture of yourself getting up early and enjoying yourself in your sketchbook.
- It can be anything, including reading a book, playing with your pet, or engaging in a hobby.
- Discuss with your parents what you have drawn and why you enjoy performing that activity in the morning.
- Include this activity in your morning routine.
- This exercise is also good for your imagination and creativity.

**Have a wonderful time!**

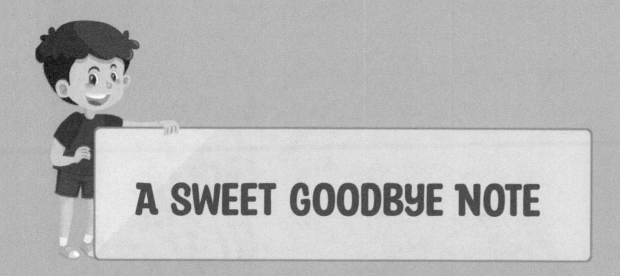

# A SWEET GOODBYE NOTE

I want to thank you for your time and say goodbye as you finish this activity book. These strategies will aid in your growth and development. You now understand the power of positive thinking. It may alter your outlook and improve the quality of your life.

You have learned to leverage your unique qualities and talents to accomplish your objectives and dreams. You have developed your ability to be mindful, making you feel more at ease, balanced, and concentrated. Also, you have learned vital social and communication abilities that will aid in developing enduring and wholesome connections with others.

Remember the life lessons you have learnt from this activity book as you go forward in your life. Continue to think positively, work from your areas of strength to accomplish your objectives, be conscious, and cultivate positive relationships with others.

Best wishes on your trip, and I hope you will keep developing and learning in each of these areas. I appreciate you coming along on this journey with me.

Made in the USA
Las Vegas, NV
05 June 2023